MODERN ROLE MODELS

Danica Patrick

Kristine Brennan

Mason Crest Publishers

Produced by OTTN Publishing in association with
21st Century Publishing and Communications, Inc.

MASON CREST PUBLISHERS INC.
370 Reed Road
Broomall, Pennsylvania 19008
(866) MCP-BOOK (toll free)
www.masoncrest.com

Printed in the United States of America.

First Printing

9 8 7 6 5 4 3 2 1

Library of Congress Cataloging-in-Publication Data

Brennan, Kristine, 1969–
    Danica Patrick / Kristine Brennan.—1st printing.
        p. cm. — (Modern role models)
    ISBN 978-1-4222-0487-0 (hardcover) — ISBN 978-1-4222-0775-8 (pbk.)
    1. Patrick, Danica, 1982–   —Juvenile literature. 2. Automobile racing drivers—
United States—Biography—Juvenile literature. 3. Women automobile racing
drivers—United States—Biography—Juvenile literature. I. Title.
GV1032.P38B74 2008
796.72092—dc22
[B]   2008025060

Publisher's note:
All quotations in this book come from original sources, and contain the spelling
and grammatical inconsistencies of the original text.

CROSS-CURRENTS

*In the ebb and flow of the currents of life we are each influenced
by many people, places, and events that we directly experience
or have learned about. Throughout the chapters of this book you
will come across CROSS-CURRENTS reference boxes. These
boxes direct you to a CROSS-CURRENTS section in the back
of the book that contains fascinating and informative sidebars
and related pictures. Go on.* ▸▸

CONTENTS

Danica Patrick holds a check for $2,500, which she received for turning in the fastest lap at the final practice session before the 2005 Indianapolis 500 race, May 27, 2005. Two days later, Danica would thrill fans at the Indianapolis Motor Speedway by contending for one of auto racing's biggest prizes.

A Superstar on Wheels

EACH YEAR, DURING MEMORIAL DAY WEEKEND, some 300,000 fans of auto racing gather at the Indianapolis Motor Speedway. Around the country, millions more tune in to watch what has been dubbed "The Greatest Spectacle in Racing." The Indianapolis 500-Mile Race, which has been run since 1911, draws 33 of the best drivers in the United States and the world.

⇛ A LADY AMONG GENTLEMEN ⇚

At 1 P.M. on Sunday, May 29, 2005, Mari Hulman George delivered the Indy 500's traditional starting announcement. But this year, George—chairperson of the Indianapolis Motor Speedway—had to alter the command slightly. "Lady and gentlemen," she called enthusiastically to the drivers, "start your engines!"

CROSS-CURRENTS

To learn about the famous racetrack in Indianapolis, as well as its biggest event, read "The Brickyard and the Indy 500." Go to page 48. ▶▶

The lady in question was a 23-year-old rookie named Danica Patrick. Danica had competed in only four other IndyCar Championship Series races, but her skills were sharp from years of driving in **developmental races**. She knew she would have to keep her cool to perform well. But the pressure was on. This was the showcase event of the **Indy Racing League (IRL)**, and fans were especially excited about seeing a promising if untested female driver perform.

⇝ PROVING HERSELF ⇜

Danica did not disappoint. On lap 56—the Indy 500 is 200 laps around the 2.5-mile track—she pulled into the lead. It was the first time a female driver had ever led the fabled race.

Danica dropped back quickly, but she was determined to return to the front. Danica had less experience than most of the other drivers, and she did make some errors. On lap 78 she stalled her car on her way out of the **pits**, causing her to drop from 4th place to 16th.

Danica battled back into the top 10, but bad luck then struck. On lap 155, during a yellow flag—a caution flag that signals drivers to slow down and stop fighting for place while a hazard on the track is taken care of—Danica spun her car into the middle of the track.

Thomas Enge's car clipped Danica's, breaking off the left front wing, which landed on the track.

Enge had to leave the race. So did another driver, Tomas Scheckter, who hit the wall trying to avoid Danica's broken wing. Luckily for Danica, one minute in the pits was all it took to repair her car. She cruised along under the yellow flag for four laps, and then took another pit stop to refuel and get a new set of tires.

CROSS-CURRENTS

To find out more about the high-powered autos in which Danica races, check out "Indy Cars." Go to page 49. ▸▸

The drivers ahead of her went in to get fuel and new tires at lap 172. Danica, team owner Bobby Rahal, and her pit crew decided to take a chance. She would stay out of the pits for the rest of the race and try to take the lead while the other leaders refueled.

On lap 172, she recalled in her autobiography, *Danica: Crossing the Line*:

❝I found myself in the position I had hoped for, dreamed of, and wanted so much—I was in the lead for the second time that day.❞

Driving car number 16 for Rahal Letterman Racing, Danica Patrick takes the lead on lap 172 of the 2005 Indianapolis 500. It was the first time in the 89-year history of the race that a woman had ever led. Danica would hold the lead for a total of 19 laps. The race was eventually won by Dan Wheldon.

She hung on until lap 185, thrilling the crowd. Because the race is so long, however, drivers must pace themselves and keep an eye on their fuel supply. Close communication with the pit crew is vital. The rest of the Indy 500 would require Danica to use her remaining fuel wisely if she wanted to stay ahead without running out of gas.

Dan Wheldon edged by her on lap 186. She was critically low on fuel, but a yellow flag allowed her to conserve it without losing her position in the race. When the green flag came back out, signaling the resumption of the race in earnest, Danica took a risk to try to win it all. She poured it on in the restart and took the lead back

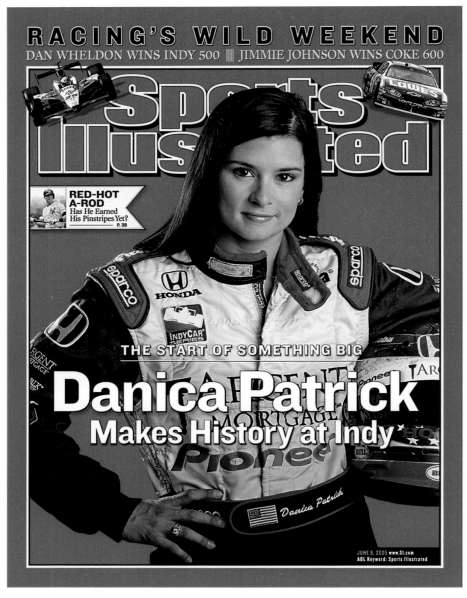

Danica's fourth-place finish at Indianapolis—the best ever by a female racer—landed her on the cover of *Sports Illustrated*. Some of her fellow competitors grumbled at the attention the 23-year-old was getting. But there was no denying that Danica brought a new level of excitement to the Indy Racing League.

from Wheldon. It lasted for three more laps—but six laps remained in the race.

Wheldon passed her again. If she wanted to finish the Indy 500, Danica would have to back off on speed and save what little fuel she had left. That gave two other drivers, Vitor Meira and Bryan Herta, a chance to overtake Danica as well. She finished fourth in an exciting race.

At first, Danica was a little disappointed because she had come close to winning. She had gone to the Indianapolis 500 to place first—not fourth. But nearly everyone else was astonished by her achievement. In only her fifth IRL race, Danica had led the Indy 500 for 19 laps. No other female racer had ever come close to this feat.

➤ OVERNIGHT SENSATION ◆

Dan Wheldon won the 89th Indianapolis 500, yet it seemed that all eyes were trained on the fourth-place finisher. A *Sports Illustrated* cover featuring Danica with the headline "The Start of Something Big: Danica Patrick Makes History at Indy" appeared that week. It was the first time in 20 years that *SI* had featured an IRL driver on its cover.

She may not have won, but Danica got the lion's share of attention after the Indianapolis 500. In her No. 16 Argent Mortgage/Pioneer Honda Panoz car, Danica Patrick had become a superstar on wheels and boosted the profile of her team, Rahal Letterman Racing.

Danica used her newfound fame to raise some money for charity. In an online auction, her broken left front wing netted $42,650.01 for Best Buddies Indiana, an organization that helps people with intellectual disabilities. Danica autographed the wing and joined forces with her team and with Thomas Enge, the other driver in the accident, and his team, Panther Racing, to present it to the auction winner.

Danica Patrick had become an overnight sensation. But getting to this point had taken years of hard work and determination.

Danica Patrick poses in front of a Formula One race car. Since childhood, racing has been Danica's passion. At age 10 she was a dedicated go-kart driver. By high school she would leave her home in Illinois and move to England so that she could drive in the Formula Vauxhall developmental circuit there.

Born to Drive

ALMOST FROM HER BIRTH ON MARCH 25, 1982, in Beloit, Wisconsin, Danica Sue Patrick seemed destined to become a racer. It was in her blood: Her father, T. J., and her mother, Bev, met at a snowmobile race in 1978. He was a competitor and she was another racer's mechanic. T. J. also raced midget cars and motocross bikes.

The Patricks were an active, hardworking family. T. J. and Bev started a successful plate glass company out of their home in Roscoe, Illinois. Bev handled the company's finances while caring for Danica and her younger sister, Brooke.

It was Brooke's idea to try go-karting. T. J. and Bev Patrick bought their daughters karts. A go-kart designed for the track has a five-horsepower engine and no **suspension**. Brooke soon got tired of karting, but Danica could never get enough time at nearby Sugar River Raceway.

By the time she was 10, piloting her first go-kart was her passion. She wrote in her autobiography:

> **"Instead of playing soccer after school or taking piano lessons, I dedicated myself to becoming the best racecar driver in the world."**

She stood out from the field of boys in a bright purple-and-green racing suit. Danica finished her very first season of karting with frequent wins.

CROSS-CURRENTS

If you'd like to learn more about the sport of karting, check out "Danica's First Ride: A Go-Kart." Go to page 50. ▶▶

Local wins soon became regional wins, then national wins. During racing season, weekends were spent driving to distant tracks, racing, and then hurrying home. Danica was grateful to Brooke and her parents for committing so much time and effort to helping her achieve her dreams. Her family was her original pit crew and cheering section.

Her first crash occurred when Danica was 12 years old. The driver she hit that day was a boy named Sam Hornish Jr.—future winner of the 2006 Indy 500 and one of IndyCar racing's premier drivers before he moved to NASCAR in 2008. Both young drivers were unhurt.

In high school, Danica knew that she was driving the karts too hard and it was time to move on to a race car. She also needed to make a lasting commitment to racing. In the 10th grade, she lost her spot on the high school cheerleading squad because driving conflicted too much with practices and games. Unlike many high school students, Danica already knew what she wanted to do with her life. Now, she needed to take her next big step.

⇒ ON HER OWN IN ENGLAND ⇐

Danica Patrick finished her karting career with multiple national championships. She did something bold to begin the next leg of her journey to professional racing. Danica went to Milton Keynes, England, to drive in England's rough-and-tumble **open-wheel** developmental races. It was a decision that involved many sacrifices. It meant going abroad alone and taking **General Educational Development (GED)** tests while her friends back home in the

United States graduated from high school without her. It also meant living far from home without her parents to guide her. In her autobiography, Danica recalled the factors that had gone into her decision to leave home:

> **❝I had no idea what I was getting myself into, but I had to listen to my gut and just go for it. ❞**

For Bev and T. J. Patrick, allowing Danica to go to England meant trusting their daughter's judgment and investing a lot of money in her future. Fortunately, a Texas family with great interest in auto racing agreed to help them pay for her training in England.

In 1998 Danica raced a partial season in the Formula Vauxhall circuit. She wrecked her car in her very first Vauxhall race. Staying focused on her driving was hard because she was lonely. At first, she had only a couch to sleep on; later, she got a tiny bedroom. The young drivers in England were so competitive that she found it difficult to make any real friends. In addition, the mechanics and engineers she was forced to depend on didn't seem very interested in helping Danica drive the best car possible.

CROSS-CURRENTS

To find out how young drivers like Danica learn to race professionally, read "Driver Development." Go to page 51. ▶▶

She was relieved to go home over Christmas. Danica got a job, prepared for her GED exam and spent her free time with friends. Although she was enjoying normal teenage activities at home, her parents noticed that their daughter's attitude had a new, hard edge. She stayed out very late with her friends, and T. J. and Bev grounded her for it.

Soon, Danica's sponsors from Texas called to withdraw their support. They were told that the young driver they were sponsoring had been partying too much.

The Patricks got tough with their daughter, forcing her to take full responsibility for her actions. It fell on Danica's shoulders to call her sponsors and beg for one more chance in England. They finally agreed, but they were still angry. At home, Danica buckled down, working out regularly and striving to regain her parents' trust before she went back to England for the 1999 Vauxhall season.

She finished the series ninth in the points standings. She graduated to the Formula Ford Series in 2000. Another driver before her had

Danica and her mother, Bev, talk before a practice session. The two have a very close relationship, and Bev has always supported her daughter's career choices. When asked once by a reporter about what it was like to have a daughter in the male-dominated world of auto racing, Bev Patrick responded, "Well, the car doesn't know the difference."

used her car's **chassis**. Danica likened driving a car made of mostly hand-me-down parts to playing baseball with a borrowed glove.

Danica has often referred to England as a crucial test of her mental toughness. She faced stiff competition, beat-up equipment, and a lot of hostility just because she was female. But Danica's 2000 season with the Haywood Racing Team also gave her a taste of better times to come. In her autobiography, she remembered one special race:

> **"Even though it rained the whole weekend, my heart, if only for a moment, was filled with sunshine."**

She drove to a second-place finish in the Formula Ford Festival. Hers was the best showing ever by an American in that race. She had overcome hardships and mistakes to become a rising star in open-wheel racing. She was sure that she would now attract a helpful pit crew and better cars.

Yet nothing really changed. Danica believed she was driving as well or better than the young men in England, but she wasn't getting credit for her hard work. She left England in 2001 after doing something drastic. Disgusted by the lack of support her team was giving her, Danica called her sponsors for help. They told her to sit out an upcoming race to make a statement to Haywood Racing's owners.

She took this advice, even though she had never skipped a race in her whole career, and she felt unsportsmanlike and petty for doing so. Her association with Haywood came to an abrupt end. Her sister, Brooke, traveled to England to accompany Danica home for the last time.

⇒ BACK IN THE UNITED STATES ⇐

Although her time in England ended on a sour note, Danica had grown as a driver. She had her Formula Ford Festival podium finish to show for it, and she also won the Gorsline Human Performance Institute Scholarship for 2002. This was awarded each year to a talented, up-and-coming race car driver.

Happy as she was to be home, Danica needed a position with a new team. She spent many weekends at racetracks, shaking hands and asking to **test-drive** cars for a lot of team owners. Despite her achievements in England, Danica had a hard time. She began to doubt that she'd ever get her chance to show what she could do behind the wheel.

Bobby Rahal, owner of Rahal Racing (later Rahal Letterman Racing), was a legend. One of his many accomplishments was winning the 1986 Indy 500. He had been quietly taking note of Danica's progress. Rahal admired her for being brave enough to go to England at such a young age. He had trained there during his twenties, so he understood how tough it must have been for her.

All Danica Patrick needed was a chance to show her stuff in the United States. Would Rahal be her ticket to ride?

Before Danica Patrick got a chance to drive against top-level competition in the IndyCar Championship Series, she had to prove herself in developmental races. In 2002 she became the first woman to win the professional division of the Toyota Pro/Celebrity Race in Long Beach, California. In 2003 she captured 10 top-10 finishes in the Toyota Atlantic Championship Series.

Making the Big Leagues

DANICA PATRICK WAS TIRED OF GOING TO SPEED-
ways as a spectator. What she really wanted was to
race at the highest levels. She knew Bobby Rahal
considered her a promising driver: he had arranged a
few test-drives for her. If she could rack up some good
finishes in developmental races, maybe he'd give her a
shot at the big time.

Danica's first American developmental program was with Rahal
Racing in the Barber Dodge Pro Series. She competed in five races,
including the 2002 Toyota Pro/Celebrity Race, held in Long Beach,
California. This race is unique because it has two divisions: one for
professional drivers from all different kinds of automotive racing;
and one for celebrities, who undergo three days of intensive training
and advice from pro drivers before the event.

By 2002 the Toyota Pro/Celebrity Race was in its 32nd year, and it
attracted a great deal of interest—from die-hard fans of auto racing

as well as fans who were more interested in catching a glimpse of some of their favorite stars from the entertainment industry. Over the years, celebrity drivers have included such Hollywood luminaries as Clint Eastwood and Cameron Diaz.

At the 2002 event, Olympic swimmer Dara Torres became the first woman ever to win the celebrity division. But girl power reigned completely that year: Danica Patrick bested the competition to become the first woman ever to win in the professional division. Danica's victory in Long Beach created quite a buzz for the young driver—just the kind of publicity she was hoping would help sway Bobby Rahal to give her a chance to prove her mettle against top-level drivers.

In 2003 Danica raced in the Toyota Atlantic Championship Series as part of Rahal's team. This series features races in the United States, Canada, and Mexico. It was in Monterrey, Mexico, that Danica became the first woman to reach the podium in a Toyota Atlantic event. She finished third.

In 12 Toyota Atlantic races in 2003, Danica logged top-10 finishes 10 times. She saved her best performance for the season finale, which was held in Miami on September 28. That day, Danica raced to a second-place finish. This excellent showing ensured that she ended up sixth in the overall Toyota Atlantic standings.

In the 2004 season, Danica improved her rank in the overall standings to third. She accomplished another first for a woman racing in the Toyota Atlantic Championship Series when she captured **pole position** at the race in Portland. She made it to the podium three times, including a repeat third-place finish at Monterrey. Over the course of the season, Danica raced at a consistently high level. She led all Toyota Atlantic drivers with a total of 10 finishes in the top five.

⮆ IRL ROOKIE SEASON ⮜

Danica's consistent performance led Bobby Rahal to bump her up to the IndyCar Championship Series for the 2005 season. At the age of 23, she had made the big leagues. She was grateful to Rahal, and she wanted to prove to him that he had been right to take her on when no one else would. But most of all, she couldn't wait to compete with some of open-wheel racing's best drivers.

Danica would drive the No. 16 Argent Mortgage Pioneer Honda Panoz Firestone car. The first event of the season was the Toyota

Cameras and microphones surround Danica Patrick and her crew chief before a race. Even as an Indy Racing League rookie with no victories under her belt, Danica drew a huge amount of media attention. Reporters and photographers seemed to follow her every move.

Indy 300, run at Florida's Homestead-Miami Speedway on March 6. During qualifying, Danica earned the ninth starting position. For 158 of the race's 200 laps, she ran strongly, keeping in the front half of the field. On lap 159, however, she tried to avoid getting caught in an eight-car pileup and crashed into a wall. Her car bounced into the infield before coming to a stop. It wasn't exactly the way Danica had hoped her IndyCar debut would turn out.

In addition to ending her race, the crash sent Danica to the hospital with a concussion. After a few hours of treatment and observation, however, the doctors released the young driver.

Crashes are an occupational hazard of auto racing, and Danica has seen her share. In fact, her IRL debut—on March 6, 2005, at the Toyota Indy 300 at Homestead-Miami Speedway—was ended prematurely by an eight-car pileup. Danica's car careened off a wall and spun into the infield. The crash sent her to the hospital with a concussion.

The lingering effects of a concussion can include headaches, blurred vision, and impaired balance—symptoms that would certainly prevent a race car driver from getting behind the wheel. But the next race in the IndyCar Championship Series was coming up in just two weeks, and Danica didn't want to miss it. She spent most of the two weeks resting and using old-fashioned icepacks and a few newer therapies to get her body ready to race again. These included wearing electrical muscle stimulation pads all over her body. An earpiece and goggles gave Danica light and sound therapy.

CROSS-CURRENTS

To learn about safety features that have been incorporated into many motor speedways to protect drivers, read "Making Speed SAFER." Go to page 51. ▶▶

As her body mended, Danica's mechanics and engineers worked on fixing her car. By the time of the next race—the XM Satellite Radio Indy 200 in Danica's new hometown of Phoenix—both driver and car were ready to go. But the car didn't handle the way Danica wanted it to. Still, she finished the race in 15th place after a starting position of 18th.

Danica improved at the next race, the Honda Grand Prix of St. Petersburg. In that event—held April 3 in St. Petersburg, Florida—she finished 12th.

The next event was the Indy Japan 300. It was run at Twin Ring Motegi in Motegi, Japan, on April 30—less than a month before the Indy 500. Danica's driving at Motegi hinted at the great performance to come. She qualified second; her old go-kart rival Sam Hornish Jr. captured the pole. Danica led for a total of 32 laps and finished in fourth place. Danica and her crew did a good job of staying at the front of the pack without running out of gas—a constant balancing act in racing.

Danica's performance at Motegi only raised everyone's expectations of her. During the month of May, throngs of people wanted to interview her. It was draining, but she found comfort in having her family with her as she got ready for the big day.

⇒ INDY 500 AFTERMATH ⇐

Danica Patrick's groundbreaking fourth-place finish at the Indy 500 landed her on the cover of *Sports Illustrated*, and "Danica mania" grew. She basked in glowing press coverage. Dick Mittman, writing on the Indianapolis Motor Speedway's official Web site, observed:

> **"**Daniel Clive Wheldon of Emberton, England, won the most famous race in the world on May 29 at the Indianapolis Motor Speedway.
>
> But Danica Patrick, a black-haired girl from America's heartland, captured the hearts of America from sea to shining sea by nearly winning the race and making it clear that a female can race with the boys and battle them wheel to wheel to the very last lap.**"**

Dan Wheldon became exasperated that the limelight shone not on him but on the fourth-place finisher. He showed up at the next IRL race (the Bombardier Learjet 500, held at Texas Motor Speedway in Fort Worth) wearing a T-shirt that read, "I actually won the Indy 500."

Nevertheless, the fevered publicity surrounding Danica continued, even though she was mediocre in her next two races. But then she turned in the fastest qualifying time at Kansas Speedway, thereby capturing the pole position for the July 3 running of the Argent Mortgage Indy 300. She was the second woman in IRL history to win a pole in an IndyCar event, after Sarah Fisher. In the race, Danica finished ninth, one spot ahead of teammate Buddy Rice.

She led for several laps at the Firestone Indy 200 in Nashville, Tennessee. But she ended up finishing in seventh place. Yet the buzz continued.

"Danica mania" began to bother some of her competitors. Four drivers from Andretti Green Racing were fined by the IRL when they refused to attend an autograph session at the Milwaukee Mile because they were sick and tired of seeing Danica held up as the face of the IndyCar series.

⇾ UPS AND DOWNS ⇽

Bad luck caught up with Danica on July 24 at the ABC Supply/A.J. Foyt 225. It was extremely hot, making the Milwaukee Mile's oval track slippery. Danica crashed on lap 125 and didn't finish. Misfortune struck again the following week at Michigan International Speedway, when mechanical problems ended her chances of winning the Firestone Indy 400.

Danica pulls on her gloves before a race. A racer's helmet, fire suit, and gloves are designed to protect in the event of a crash or fire. In addition, Indy cars have a variety of safety features. But there is no way to fully protect a driver traveling at speeds in excess of 220 miles per hour.

Things started out better at her next race, with Danica winning the pole at Kentucky Speedway for the AMBER Alert Portal Indy 300 on August 14. After her first pit stop, though, things went downhill. Car trouble pulled her down to a 16th-place finish.

She rebounded with an eighth-place finish at the Honda Indy 225 on August 21. A week later, however, a three-car crash on lap 18 eliminated Danica from the Argent Mortgage Indy Grand Prix.

On September 11, Danica found herself back in the top 10 at Chicagoland Speedway. She finished the PEAK Antifreeze Indy 300 in sixth place after capturing the pole. Her next race saw her back

This poster, an advertisement for Rahal Letterman Racing sponsor Argent Mortgage, celebrated Danica Patrick's winning of IRL Rookie of the Year honors for 2005. As a woman succeeding in a sport dominated by men—and especially as an attractive woman—Danica would prove to be an advertiser's dream.

down in 16th place at Watkins Glen International in Watkins Glen, New York. She made an error that damaged her car, but she still managed to finish the road course.

Her performance at Watkins Glen was good enough for Danica to walk away with the Bombardier Learjet Rookie of the Year title for 2005. She hoped that she could end the season with a great performance in the next race.

⧁ A CRASH AND A CONFRONTATION ⧀

The final race of Danica's rookie season, the Toyota Indy 400, was held at California Speedway on October 16. Danica was running well when, on lap 184, she got caught up in a race-ending crash with Jaques Lazier.

Danica and Lazier each blamed the other for the crash. And as luck would have it, the two had to leave the track in the same rescue van. Some sort of confrontation ensued. Lazier later told reporters that Danica hit him in the rescue van.

A swirl of rumors and a war of words followed the incident. Danica later tried to set the record straight in her autobiography:

> **"Now that the dust has settled, although I did not actually slap or punch him, I can now admit that I did give his head a little help meeting the van door."**

There was no question that Danica had made quite an impression—and that she had the talent to justify the hype. But could she keep up the momentum next season?

Danica Patrick is a picture of concentration before a race. Auto racing requires intense mental focus as well as physical strength and stamina. Danica, though just five feet two inches tall and weighing only 100 pounds, is surprisingly strong. To stay fit, she runs, works out daily with weights, and does yoga.

Moving On, Moving Up

IN ADDITION TO THE MANY ACCOLADES SHE earned in 2005, Danica Patrick was named the IRL's Most Popular Driver, a distinction she would repeat in 2006 and 2007. In 2006 her fans were eager for her to build on a great rookie season. Danica, too, was excited about the prospect of building on her success.

But first, Danica Patrick took one big step that had nothing to do with driving: on November 19, 2005, she married Paul Hospenthal. The newlywed was behind the wheel again in January 2006, though. NASCAR racing legend and TV commentator Rusty Wallace asked Danica to drive on his team for the Rolex 24 Hours of Daytona. Held at Daytona International Speedway in Florida, the 24 Hours is a grueling race in which team members take shifts driving one car for 24 hours.

Danica drove a Pontiac-Crawford sports car. Her team led five laps of the race, going a total of 273 laps around the 2.5-mile track. Unfortunately, mechanical trouble prevented the team from finishing.

Danica walks the infield with her husband, Paul Hospenthal, before a 2006 race. The two met when Hospenthal, a sports trainer and physical therapist, treated Danica for an injured hip. They dated for a couple of years before he proposed, over the Thanksgiving holiday in 2004. They were married on November 19, 2005.

➤ A TRAGEDY ◀

Tragedy would cloud the season opener at Homestead-Miami Speedway on March 26. Danica qualified in the third spot at 216.798 miles per hour. During practice, however, a Rahal Letterman teammate named Paul Dana died in a horrific crash. After driver Ed Carpenter lost control of his car and went into a spin, Dana slammed into him at full speed. Carpenter walked away from the wreck with only a bruised lung. Dana, age 30, died two hours later.

Danica and teammate Buddy Rice withdrew from the race, which went on in a somber mood. Before the next event, a road race at St. Petersburg, IRL chaplain Bob Hills conducted a memorial service for Paul Dana. Danica and Rice competed this time. She started in the 14th spot and fought her way up to a sixth-place finish. Danica again started 14th at Twin Ring Motegi in Japan on April 22. She finished in eighth place.

Eighth place seemed to be reserved just for Danica after Motegi. On May 28, she finished in that spot again after starting 10th at the Indy 500. She followed that up with another eighth-place finish at Watkins Glen.

≫ A DIFFICULT YEAR ≪

After Paul Dana's fatal crash, Rahal Letterman Racing struggled to maintain good **morale**. In the middle of the 2006 season, the drivers and crews all faced mechanical woes, too. Rahal Letterman's cars had been running with Panoz chassis, but the other teams in the IRL used Dallara chassis. The Dallaras were newer and faster, so Rahal Letterman switched over, too. The move had big implications.

Unlike regular cars, Indy cars are tuned before every race to handle the unique conditions of each track or course. On an oval track, for instance, the car is set to always turn in one direction; the driver has to steer hard to make it run straight. On road courses, the car is fixed to go straight unless the driver turns hard. Everything about how the car drives can change from race to race. A new chassis meant that Danica and her crew had to start from scratch and relearn how to make her car as fast and responsive as possible.

Danica and her crew weren't having much success early in the 2006 season. She failed to break into the top 10 for three straight races. Then, at Nashville Superspeedway and the Milwaukee Mile, Danica tied her career-best performances of 2005 with a pair of fourth-place finishes.

But mechanical problems struck on July 30 at Michigan National Speedway. With just three laps remaining, Danica's car conked out, leaving her in 17th place.

Just days earlier, Danica had announced that she would make a fresh start. Rumors flew that she was going to leave the IRL for NASCAR. It turned out that she was staying in the IRL, but

Rahal Letterman Racing technicians work on Danica Patrick's car. During the 2006 season, Rahal Letterman switched from Panoz to Dallara chassis. Although Dallaras were faster, Danica's crew struggled to fine-tune her car to her liking. As a result, Danica faltered early in the 2006 season, failing to muster a top-10 finish in her first three races.

she was leaving Rahal Letterman to join Andretti Green Racing for the 2007 season.

She ended her 2006 season—and her time with Rahal Letterman—with a 12th-place finish at Chicagoland Speedway on September 10. Her overall ranking in the IRL for the year was ninth.

⇒ A New Team, a New Season ⇐

Danica thought joining Andretti Green Racing would make her more competitive on the track. Co-owners Michael Andretti and Kim Green believed in her potential. Andretti is member of the famous Andretti racing family, with 42 career wins to his credit. Danica's teammates were Tony Kanaan, Dario Franchitti, and Michael's son Marco Andretti.

The 2007 season opened at Homestead-Miami Speedway, where Danica had suffered a concussion in 2005 and Paul Dana had died in 2006. The bad luck continued, with Danica getting 14th place after an accident. She improved in the next three races, with an 11th-place finish sandwiched between two top-10 finishes.

In the run-up to the 2007 Indianapolis 500, members of Andretti Green Racing ring the opening bell for the New York Stock Exchange, a team sponsor, May 21, 2007. In front, from left: Danica Patrick, Tony Kanaan, Dario Franchitti, Marco Andretti, and Michael Andretti.

⇒ THE 2007 INDY 500 ⇐

At the 91st running of the Indy 500 on May 27, Danica finished eighth, just as she had in 2006. But this race was interrupted by a red flag because of rain after 113 laps. That was enough laps to make the race count. If continued rain had prevented the resumption of the race, Tony Kanaan would have won, followed by Marco Andretti in second and Danica in third for an Andretti Green sweep.

But the rain did let up, and positions changed when the race resumed. When Danica had to make a pit stop, she lost her spot to drivers who stayed on the track. Kanaan blew a tire after making contact with Jaques Lazier's car. Lazier crashed out; Kanaan had to settle for 12th place. Marco Andretti crashed just before it started pouring again. Danica's teammate and race leader Dario Franchitti was declared the winner, and the race was stopped after 166 laps.

CROSS-CURRENTS

To learn more about the challenges faced by female drivers, read "Racing with the Boys." Go to page 52. ▶▶

The drama of the actual race overshadowed the pre-race hype that had surrounded Danica and fellow Indy 500 qualifiers Sarah Fisher and Milka Duno. Never before in the history of Indy had there been three female drivers in the field. Fisher finished 18th; Duno ended up in 31st after an accident.

⇒ THREE VISITS TO THE PODIUM ⇐

On June 3 the action moved from Indianapolis to the Milwaukee Mile for the ABC Supply/A.J. Foyt 225. Danica had reached fifth place a little bit less than halfway through the race when Dan Wheldon's car bumped hers. Danica spun but avoided the wall and other cars. Still, her car needed repairs, costing her time. She finished eighth.

Although Andretti Green teammate Tony Kanaan won the race, all eyes were on Danica and Wheldon. While venting at Wheldon about the crash, she appeared to give him a little shove.

On June 9, Danica put what one reporter had called the "soap opera" with Wheldon behind her. She reached the podium for the first time in her IRL career, garnering third place in the Bombardier Learjet 550K.

The IRL ran its first race at the Iowa Speedway in Newton, Iowa, on June 24. The Corn Indy 250 was good for Andretti Green, with Dario Franchitti and Marco Andretti finishing in first and second,

Action from the 91st Indianapolis 500, May 27, 2007. Because of bad weather, the race had to be called after just 166 laps. An ill-timed pit stop cost Danica a chance to finish on the podium, but her Andretti Green teammate Dario Franchitti won the rain-shortened event.

respectively. But Danica did not share in her teammates' glory that day. She made contact with both Ed Carpenter and A. J. Foyt IV. Kosuke Matsuura hit a wall while trying to keep clear of them. Danica finished 13th in a race filled with crashes.

On July 15 at Nashville Superspeedway, Danica snagged another third-place finish in the Firestone Indy 200. In the hunt for first, Danica was frustrated when Ed Carpenter, running a lap behind her, seemed unwilling to let her get around his car. Her complaints about Carpenter's driving were quoted in *USA Today*:

❛❛You just look stupid when you play a role in the leaders' race. I would feel dumb, personally.❜❜

Carpenter said he was trying to avoid spinning on debris that had built up on the track. Annoyed that people blamed him for interfering with Danica, he said:

❛❛I've never had so many people call me unsportsmanlike after a race. I didn't expect this to turn into such a big deal, but it happens when Danica is involved.❜❜

Most of Danica's races that followed this dustup proved to be big deals: three top-10 finishes, marred by one 16th-place result after an accident at Kentucky Speedway on August 11.

On September 2, Danica had her best IRL finish at The Raceway at Belle Isle in Detroit, a street circuit. She placed second in the event, which Tony Kanaan won.

Danica's last race of 2007 was at Chicagoland. She finished in 11th place, which was good enough for her to end the season seventh in the points standings with a total of 424. She was also voted the IRL's Most Popular Driver for the third time in a row.

The TV ads, print ads, and photo shoots kept coming. In a way, Ed Carpenter was right: Danica still caused a stir just by showing up somewhere. She fueled the spotlight during the off-season. A TV commercial that aired during Super Bowl XLII, and pictures in *Sports Illustrated's* 2008 Swimsuit Issue, were just two of the ways Danica used her beauty and her fame to promote herself and her sport.

➤ LOOKING AHEAD ➤

Danica was excited by other off-season developments. In 1995 open-wheel racing had divided into rival leagues: the IRL and the Champ Car Series. Both leagues suffered when the fan base was split into two. On February 22, 2008, Champ Car co-owners Kevin Kalkhoven and Gerald Forsythe and IRL founder Tony George signed a deal that would absorb Champ Car into the IRL. They would begin racing together right away: the 2008 IRL season was going to start in several weeks.

Danica Patrick and Tony Kanaan shower each other with champagne, September 2, 2007. The Andretti Green team-mates were celebrating their performances at the Detroit Belle Island Grand Prix. Danica finished second in the three-day race, which was her career-best showing in an IndyCar event; Kanaan won.

Fans and drivers alike praised reunification. It promised more cars and more competition, as well as a bigger fan base. Danica weighed in on the merger during an interview:

❝We're going to get great races put together. We're going to have all the best events put into one series, and more drivers, and that always makes for more passing, more excitement, more interest. So it's a win, win, win, win situation.❞

Danica Patrick in a publicity photo. Danica is living her dream, making a lot of money doing what she loves best. But auto racing is by no means the only important thing in her life. Danica tries to balance her career with her family life and other non-racing interests.

A Life on Track

FOR YEARS DANICA PATRICK HAS BEEN EATING, sleeping, and breathing auto racing. Her single-minded dedication has certainly paid off. Danica is living her dream, competing and succeeding at the highest levels of Indy car racing. But that is not to say racing is the only important thing in her life.

Danica shares her triumphs and setbacks with her husband, Paul Hospenthal. Danica had her morning yoga routine to thank for helping her find a soul mate. In 2002 she injured her hip doing yoga. Bobby Rahal, Danica's team owner at the time, was friends with Hospenthal, a physical therapist. So he made an appointment with his friend for a young driver named "Danny."

When Hospenthal saw Danica in the waiting room of his Phoenix office, he wondered whether she was the injured driver's girlfriend. He quickly realized his mistake, and Danica appreciated her new physical therapist's sense of humor. After her treatment, Danica took him out to dinner to thank him for staying late to see her. They struck up a friendship and saw each other when Danica was available.

Gradually, a romance blossomed. Hospenthal proposed during a Thanksgiving visit with Danica's family in 2004.

Danica's marriage has helped her enjoy life off the track as much as she loves being a driver. In her autobiography, she revealed that her husband and family gave her a sense of being at home no matter where racing took her:

> **"These days I don't have to worry about navigating the course alone because my husband is with me, by my side, making this journey with me. I will never be alone again—and what a feeling that is."**

⋙ TELLING HER STORY ⋘

Danica: Crossing the Line was published in 2006. She had just completed her celebrated rookie season and was still a very young woman, but that didn't stop Danica from writing an autobiography. She had already been pursuing her racing dream for more than a decade. She had chased her goals through some pretty tough times, too. She hoped that her example would inspire other young people, especially girls, to ignore their critics and enjoy the traits that make them stand out from the crowd.

CROSS-CURRENTS

If you'd like to learn more about some other female drivers, check out "Women in Racing." Go to page 54. ▶▶

After all, it had worked for her—even in England, when she was all alone with no real friends or mentors. Now, she was feeling confident and she wanted to share that feeling with her younger fans.

⋙ MAKING CHOICES ⋘

Around the time Danica's autobiography was released, she was contemplating serious changes in her career. She considered moving to the NASCAR Sprint Cup Series. Her father and manager, T. J. Patrick, reportedly attended a NASCAR race and talked with representatives of a racing team. In the end, however, Danica decided to stay put. She hadn't accomplished everything she wanted in the IRL. She had not yet won a single race, much less stood on the victor's podium at the Indianapolis 500. In addition, while she appreciated

Role model: As a young fan looks on, Danica signs a copy of her 2006 autobiography, *Danica: Crossing the Line*. Danica said that in writing the book she wanted "to show anyone trying to succeed that anything is possible and that, though being a woman might describe me, it doesn't define who I am on or off the track."

the enthusiasm of NASCAR fans, the stock car racing schedule is grueling, with more than twice the number of events each season as the IRL. Danica didn't want her life away from the track to suffer.

She did, however, make the decision to move to another IRL team, leaving Bobby Rahal behind to join Andretti Green Racing for the 2007 season. At a press conference on July 26, 2006, Danica acknowledged all that Rahal had done for her:

> **❝I've had a very good run, a very good relationship with Rahal Letterman and Bobby Rahal. He helped me when no one else stepped up. And I will be forever grateful for that. ❞**

⟫ GIVING BACK ⟪

In the months and years after her breakout performance at Indianapolis, Danica grew into a spokesperson for her sport. She could be fiery at the track, but she was a poised interviewee who looked good on camera.

Danica has donated her time and talents for a variety of charitable causes. Here she poses for a photograph at a fund-raising event for the Foundation for Cancer Research, New York City, 2006. A fan of glamorous clothes, makeup, and jewelry, Danica especially likes dressing up for a good cause.

Danica's fame also gave her opportunities to give back to the community. She took time to visit children's hospitals, chatting with and signing autographs for the kids and their parents. She joined other popular drivers for a 2007 event aimed at helping kids: the Michael Andretti Foundation Gala to Benefit the Children of St. Petersburg. Danica donated a racing suit for the charity auction and attended the event. The money that was raised went to groups promoting the health, education, and safety of children living in St. Petersburg, Florida.

A fan of glamorous clothes and makeup off the track, Danica sometimes dresses up for good causes. Fashion Week in February 2007 gave her one such chance. Fashion Week is a twice-yearly event held in New York City's Bryant Park for fashion designers to show off their latest creations. Danica was a model for a day, walking the runway in a red designer dress along with other celebrities. She was in the Heart Truth Show—an event sponsored by the Red Dress Project, an organization dedicated to promoting heart-disease prevention and treatment for women.

When Phoenix hosted the Super Bowl in 2008, actress Holly Robinson-Peete and her husband, former NFL quarterback Rodney Peete, coordinated a celebrity fashion show and auction in the city to benefit their HollyRod Foundation, which helps people live well with Parkinson's disease. The event also benefited the Southwest Autism Research & Resource Center (SAARC). Danica was on hand to lend her support. Before she walked the runway for the 10th Annual Gridiron Glamour event, Danica told *Access Hollywood*:

> **"I don't know if I'll be any good at it, but I'll rock what I've got."**

⇒ STRIKING POSES ⇐

Danica Patrick's popularity extends well beyond fans of racing. Danica has become a crossover celebrity. Her fame is due in part to her success in a field long dominated by men. But Danica's beauty has unquestionably also played a major role. Her long, dark hair, bright smile, and athletic figure—along with her racing talent—have combined to make her a sought-after spokesperson for a range of companies. Danica's **endorsement** deals have made her millions of

An ad for the Swiss watchmaking company Tissot. Danica has parlayed her beauty and her intriguing story into a variety of lucrative endorsement deals. "She transcends the sport of motor racing," one marketing director observed. "She's very iconic. . . . You don't have to watch Indy Racing to know who Danica Patrick is."

Racer with a million-watt smile, 2007. By that year, Danica had made the Forbes Celebrity 100 list. According to the editors, she ranked as the 95th most influential and best-paid celebrity. Her income was estimated at $5 million. Only four female athletes ranked ahead of her on the list: tennis players Maria Sharapova and Serena Williams, and golfers Michelle Wie and Annika Sorenstam.

dollars. In fact, in 2007 she ranked 95th on the Forbes Celebrity 100, a list of the best-paid and most influential celebrities. And only four female athletes made more from product endorsements in 2007.

But Danica is familiar to the general public for more than her endorsements of antiperspirant, satellite radio, and cars. She appeared, along with racing legend Dale Earnhardt Jr., in the video for rapper Jay-Z's 2006 single "Show Me What You Got."

In February 2008, Danica appeared in the famous *Sports Illustrated* Swimsuit Issue in a series of poses on a beach. She told interviewer Dan Patrick:

> **"I've bared some skin before, but nothing like in this issue. I would imagine my teammates will pick on me a little bit. "**

The *Sports Illustrated* spread was actually her second experience posing for sexy pictures. In 2002 Danica posed for another spread in *FHM* magazine. At the time, she was trying to promote herself to get racing sponsorships. In her autobiography, she admitted to some jitters about posing. But after the magazine hit newsstands, she was glad she'd done it:

> **"Why not use whatever assets I have? I'm confident in myself as a driver. It's obvious I'm a girl, so why not use it as a tool? "**

Danica's critics—including some racing fans and fellow drivers—didn't always see things that way. Some resented the way she had cashed in on her good looks; they complained that, for all the hype, Danica had never even won an IRL event. She was, these critics said, first and foremost a pretty, sexy woman rather than an elite race car driver.

CROSS-CURRENTS

For more about the publicity surrounding the off-track activities of Danica and another IRL driver, read "Too Much Exposure?" Go to page 55. ▶▶

⟫ HISTORIC RACE ⟪

Danica was determined to prove her critics wrong. And on April 20, 2008, she did so. The venue was Twin Ring Motegi; the event was the Firestone IndyCar 300 at Japan.

Helio Castroneves had won pole position in the strong field. Danica, who had always liked Motegi's 1.5-mile oval track, started the race from the sixth position. Throughout the race, Danica remained near the front, never falling below eighth place.

A yellow flag came out on lap 143 of the 200-lap race, and most of the racers took the opportunity to head to the pits. Five laps later, as green-flag conditions were about to resume, Kyle Moyer, the general manager of the Andretti Green team, suggested that Danica make a pit stop to top off her fuel. That decision would pay big dividends.

On the 189th lap, Danica was in eighth place. But as the leaders entered the pits for fuel, she moved up. By lap 196 she was in second place, behind only Castroneves. Then, with just two laps to go, Danica made her move, blowing past the leader. She never looked back, finishing a little less than six seconds ahead of Castroneves for the victory. It was the first time ever that a woman had won an IndyCar race.

Danica Patrick makes a pit stop during a 2007 race. The 2007 season featured some bright spots for Danica—she recorded 11 top-10 finishes, including a second-place finish and two third-place finishes, and she ranked seventh overall in the points standings. Nevertheless, the victory that she so desperately wanted continued to elude her.

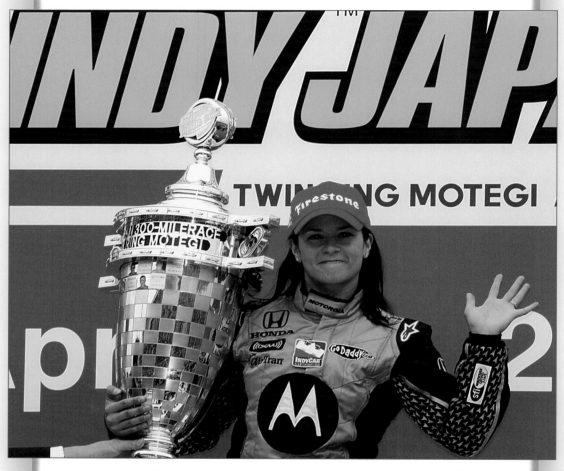

On top at last: Danica Patrick holds the winner's trophy for the Firestone IndyCar 300 at Japan, April 20, 2008. Danica's victory was the first ever for a woman in an IndyCar race. "We have all believed in her and she proved today that she is a winner," team co-owner Michael Andretti said after the race.

After the race, Castroneves complimented the winner:

❝When Danica passed me, I realized she was the leader. She did a great job, passed me fair and square and that shows you how competitive our series is.❞

For her part, Danica said she was relieved that, in her 50th IRL race, she had finally broken through for a victory:

> **That was a big relief. A long time I've waited for this. I wish it would have happened a long time ago, but I'm not going to argue with the program. It happened the way it was supposed to happen and I believe everything happens for a reason.**

As she went to the podium to accept her trophy, Danica was mobbed by her family. It was an emotional moment, and she became teary-eyed. Describing the scene, Danica told reporters:

> **There was a lot of 'I love you,' and 'congratulations.' My dad said it was the best day of his life.**

Andretti Green Racing team co-owner Michael Andretti also thought it was a pretty good day. Andretti said:

> **I'm thrilled for her that the monkey is finally off of her back. We have all believed in her and she proved today that she is a winner. Frankly, I think this is the first of many.**

"Danica maniacs" everywhere echo that sentiment.

The Brickyard and the Indy 500

Even people who don't follow automotive racing have probably heard of the Indy 500, open-wheel racing's premier event. The Indianapolis Motor Speedway, originally opened in 1909, is the biggest sports venue in the world, able to hold as many as 400,000 people. It even has its own mailing address: Speedway, Indiana, which is surrounded by the city of Indianapolis. The infield is so big it holds a golf course as well as the Indianapolis Motor Speedway Hall of Fame Museum.

Owned by Tony Hulman George, who is also the founder of the Indy Racing League, the 2.5-mile oval track was originally covered with gravel. This was soon paved over with bricks to protect drivers and spectators from debris and accidents. The speedway continues to be known as the Brickyard, even though the track is now covered with asphalt. One yard-long strip of bricks remains on the track to mark the starting/finish line.

The Indianapolis 500-Mile Race has been run nearly every year since the track was built: the only times it was cancelled were the four years that the United States was involved in World War II (1942–1945).

(Go back to page 5.) ◄◄

"The Greatest Spectacle in Racing": The Indianapolis Motor Speedway is packed for a running of the Indianapolis 500-Mile Race. The speedway—which is known to auto-racing fans as the Brickyard—is the largest sports venue in the entire world. It can hold as many as 400,000 people.

Indy Cars

Danica Patrick's car in action during a 2005 race. Indy cars are marvels of automotive technology. With their 600-horsepower engines, they are capable of accelerating from zero to 100 miles per hour in less than three seconds. Indy cars can reach speeds in excess of 225 mph.

Indy cars are not like anything your family would take for a Sunday drive! To begin, while the family roadster's engine might have an output of 160 horsepower, Indy cars boast engines of 600-plus hp. All this power enables them to accelerate from zero to 100 miles per hour in less than three seconds.

Indy cars reach speeds of more than 225 miles per hour. Even considering how skilled the drivers are, it might seem difficult to imagine how a vehicle moving so fast could be controlled. But design features and physics help keep the cars on the track.

At very high speeds, friction between tires and the surface of the track heats up the tires, causing the rubber treads to partially melt. This makes the treads sticky and helps the car stay on the track.

Indy cars also have wings. But unlike an airplane's wings, which are shaped to create lift, or upward pressure (enabling the plane to take off), an Indy car's wings are shaped to create downforce, or downward pressure. This helps keep the car on the ground.

Despite these and other design features, the speed and power of Indy cars make them very difficult to drive. It takes extensive training and great skill to race them.

(Go back to page 6.)

Danica's First Ride: A Go-Kart

Drivers line up for a go-kart race. Like Danica Patrick, some professional race car drivers have gotten their start in karts. Kids as young as eight can race karts competitively. For older racers a sanctioning body, the World Karting Association, sponsors a racing series that is scored similarly to the Indy-style racing circuits.

Danica Patrick was 10 years old when she started racing her first kart, a black, low-horsepower vehicle. (Kart engines range from 5 to 30 hp.) Karts, which are not intended to run on public streets, have no suspension. This means they have no system to keep the platform of the kart riding smoothly when the wheels jostle over bumpy surfaces. Racers as young as five years old begin to enjoy karting events, but they do not become competitive until age eight. A dedicated kart driver can advance to senior status at about 16 years of age. Karting is good preparation for professional motor sports, but it is also a fun hobby for children and adults who have no plans to drive race cars.

Danica, who was sure she wanted to become a race car driver, did most of her karting as part of the World Karting Association (WKA). Like Indy-style racing, kart racing is scored on a system that awards points for each race in a season.

By age 12, Danica Patrick had won her first national championship in the WKA. She left karting after snagging three national WKA championships during her last season in the Senior series.

(Go back to page 12.) ◀◀

Driver Development

Becoming a successful driver is not just a matter of jumping into the family car and circling a track. Karting is an excellent way for a young person to learn how to handle a vehicle built just for racing. When it is time to make the leap to cars, developmental racing teams can provide a ladder to elite race series like IndyCar, Formula One, and NASCAR. Danica Patrick raced Formula Vauxhall cars in England when she made the transition from karting to cars. Vauxhall cars are single-seat, wingless open-wheel cars with racing speeds of about 150 miles per hour. They are good preparation for Indy cars and Formula One cars, which can go well over 200 mph.

Back in the United States, Danica proved herself in the Toyota Atlantic Championship Series, an important developmental series of 12 races staged on oval tracks, road courses, and temporary street circuits.

Another open-wheel developmental series is the Indy Pro Series, launched by the IRL in 2002. Although this series is not crowded with competitors, it is meant to give aspiring Indy car drivers a chance to shine. Its main event is the Freedom 100, which is run at Indianapolis each May on the Friday before the Indy 500.

(Go back to page 13.) ◀◀

Making Speed SAFER

Danica Patrick's IRL debut on March 6, 2005, at Homestead-Miami Speedway ended with a crash into a wall. Luckily, she walked away with only a concussion. Auto racing is a dangerous sport, and some drivers have lost their lives on the track. One of Danica's own IRL teammates, Paul Dana, was killed at Homestead-Miami in a crash with another car before the first race of 2006.

The IRL and other racing organizations rely on safety features on tracks and in cars to help lower the risks. One example is the SAFER (Steel and Foam Energy Reduction) barrier. The IRL worked with experts at the University of Nebraska to create the barrier. Made of strong foam and steel, SAFER barriers were first installed on the cement walls of all four turns of the Indianapolis Motor Speedway in 2002. As of 2007, all of the oval tracks on the IndyCar Series were employing the SAFER system. Iowa Speedway has the newest version of the barrier. Iowa is also the first venue to use it all around the track, instead of just on turns. Other racing leagues now use SAFER to soften the impact of high-speed crashes.

(Go back to page 21.) ◀◀

Racing with the Boys

Automotive racing is a tough—and sometimes deadly—sport. For Danica Patrick and many women before her, its breakneck speeds and fierce competition have proven irresistible.

But auto racing has traditionally been the domain of macho men. Unfortunately, the relatively few female drivers who've aspired to big-time racing have often found it difficult to earn the respect of their mostly male competitors.

Danica Patrick was no exception. In her autobiography, *Danica: Crossing the Line*, she wrote at length about the hostility she faced while a teenager in England on the developmental racing circuit. Then, neither Danica's crew nor her team owners went out of their way to help her succeed, and at least part of the reason may have had to do with her gender. Similarly, none of the other young drivers in England befriended the girl from the United States. Despite her difficult and lonely time in England, Danica managed not just to survive, but to thrive. This says much about her toughness, resilience, and determination to excel. Now she is quite capable of dealing with occasional reminders that, as a woman, she competes in a sport that continues to be dominated by men.

Before the 2005 Indy 500, NASCAR driver Robby Gordon caused a fuss when he complained that Danica's 100-pound frame gave her an unfair edge on the track. Her car's net weight, Gordon pointed out, was considerably less than the net weight of cars driven by her bigger male competitors. He pressed the IRL to do something about this situation. When *Time* magazine later asked Danica about Gordon's comments, she replied:

> **❝I don't really have a reaction. It's just something else to cause a stir in the media. You know, Buddy Rice won with the heaviest car last year at Indy. So I'm not sure it really matters that much.❞**

Danica has also noted that, pound for pound, she has to be at least as strong as the male drivers in order to control her car against extreme gravitational pull at high speeds.

One colleague who doesn't need any convincing of Danica's ability is Rusty Wallace. A NASCAR legend who has notched 55 career victories, Wallace came away impressed after Danica drove on his Rolex 24 Hours of Daytona team in early 2006. He told ESPN.com:

> **❝I got firsthand knowledge of working with her at Daytona which proved to me she is the real deal. I've seen a lot of lady race car drivers, but she is the real deal.❞**

(Go back to page 32.) ◀◀

A woman among men: Danica Patrick (right) walks with the Scottish-born Dario Franchitti (center) and the Brazilian Helio Castroneves, May 29, 2005. The three racers were making their way to their cars before the start of the 89th Indianapolis 500. Danica would finish the race in fourth place, while Franchitti finished in sixth, and Castroneves in ninth.

Women in Racing

For almost as long as there have been automobiles, there have been fearless drivers eager to test the limits of their machines and their courage in races. Women, too, are drawn to the sport.

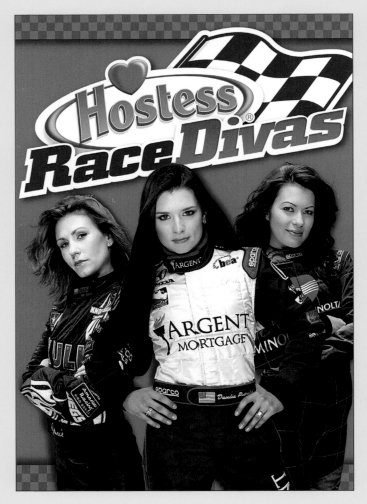

This 2007 calendar, produced by the snack manufacturer Hostess, featured three "divas" of auto racing: (from left) Melanie Troxel, Danica Patrick, and Leilani Münter. At the time, Troxel drove in the National Hot Rod Association (NHRA) drag-racing circuit. Münter was a NASCAR driver.

Kay Petre (1903–1994) was perhaps the most famous female driver of her time in England. The 4'10" racing sensation's career ended after a near-fatal crash in 1937. She later wrote about motor sports as a journalist.

The first female Formula One racer was Maria Teresa de Filippis (1926–   ). She began racing cars at the age of 22 and made her Formula One debut in 1958. The following year, she retired from racing to start a family.

The first woman to race in both the Indianapolis 500 and NASCAR's legendary Daytona 500 was Janet Guthrie (1938–   ). Her breakthrough year was 1977, when she qualified for and drove in both of these elite races. In 1978 she placed ninth in the Indy 500.

Lyn St. James (1947–   ) won Indy 500 Rookie of the Year honors in 1992, when she finished in 11th place at the age of 45. She is the founder of the Women in the Winner's Circle Foundation, teaching development classes to promising female race car drivers. Danica Patrick went through St. James's course twice.

Sarah Fisher (1980–   ) distinguished herself by

being the youngest driver—male or female—to gain admittance into the Indy Racing League. She debuted in 1999 at the age of 18. In 2000, as a member of the Walker Racing Team, Fisher became the third woman ever to compete in the Indy 500. At Kentucky Speedway, Fisher became the first woman to capture a pole position. Her 2001 second-place finish at Homestead-Miami Speedway was the best-ever finish by a woman in Indy-style racing: her record was unmatched until 2007, when Danica Patrick finished second in Detroit. Sarah Fisher left the IRL from 2004 to 2005 to drive stock cars, but returned to Indy-style racing in 2006.

Venezuelan-born driver Milka Duno (1972–) finished second with her team in the endurance race called the 24 Hours of Daytona, making hers the best finish by a woman in the history of the event. In 2007 she joined Danica Patrick and Sarah Fisher at the Indianapolis Motor Speedway for the 91st Indy 500. It was the first time a trio of women had participated in the event, but a crash on lap 65 ended Duno's day.

(Go back to page 38.) ◀◀

Too Much Exposure?

Ever since her 2002 spread in *FHM* magazine, Danica Patrick has been unafraid of using her good looks to promote her career and her sport. But can she be both a pinup girl and a serious racer?

Janet Guthrie, the first woman to drive in both the Indy 500 and NASCAR's Daytona 500, thinks that many female race car drivers feel that Patrick diminishes their credibility as athletes by posing for sexy photos. She told *USA Today*:

❝You might call it old-fashioned, but most of us wanted to be judged on the basis of what we accomplished [rather] than how we looked. I'm sure she does, too, but she's not been reluctant to take advantage of her marketable good looks.❞

Danica believes that the attention her steamy photos attract also increases interest in the IRL.

Another IRL driver, two-time Indy 500 champ Helio Castroneves, appeared on the wildly popular ABC TV show *Dancing with the Stars* in late 2007. Castroneves and his partner on the show, a professional dancer, pulled off complicated ballroom dance routines and won the competition.

It remains to be seen whether Danica Patrick's glamour photos or Helio Castroneves's charming on-camera presence will boost IRL interest and attendance. Danica isn't worried about her critics, though.

(Go back to page 44.) ◀◀

1982   Danica Sue Patrick is born on March 25 in Beloit, Wisconsin.

1992   Begins racing go-karts.

1997   Wins her last of three national karting championships.

1998   Goes to England to race in developmental open-wheel series.

2001   After returning to the United States, receives the Gorsline Human Research Institute Scholarship as a promising driver.

2002   Joins Team Rahal (later Rahal Letterman Racing) and runs an abbreviated schedule of races. Drives a sports car in the 2002 Long Beach Grand Prix Pro/Celebrity Race, winning the pro division.

2003   Races her first season in the Toyota Atlantic Series. Becomes the first female driver in the series to reach the podium when she comes in third at Monterrey, Mexico.

2004   Repeats her third-place finish at Monterrey, and reaches the podium in two other Toyota Atlantic Series events. Learns that Rahal will move her to the IRL in 2005.

2005   Achieves worldwide fame with a fourth-place finish at Indianapolis 500 on May 29, landing on the cover of *Sports Illustrated* the following week. Is named Rookie of the Year for both the Indianapolis 500 and the IndyCar Series. Marries her former physical therapist, Paul Hospenthal, on November 19.

2006   Signs with Andretti Green Racing in July, but finishes season with Rahal Letterman. Ranks ninth in total points for IndyCar Championship Series.

2007   Comes in second on September 2 at the Detroit Belle Island Grand Prix—making her the second woman to post a second-place finish in Indy-style racing (after Sarah Fisher). Also garners two third-place finishes during season. Finishes season seventh in IndyCar Championship Series rankings.

2008   Appears in the *Sports Illustrated* Swimsuit 2008 edition. Becomes first woman ever to win an IRL race, finishing first at the Firestone IndyCar 300 at Japan.

1997 World Karting Association Grand National Champion, HPV class and Yamaha Lite class
World Karting Association Summer National Champion, Yamaha Lite class

2002 Gorsline Human Performance Institute Scholarship

2004 Argent Mortgage Most Laps Completed Award

2005 Bombardier IRL IndyCar Rookie of the Year
JPMorgan Chase Indianapolis 500 Rookie of the Year
Most Popular Driver in IRL

2006 Most Popular Driver in IRL

2007 Most Popular Driver in IRL

2008 Winner, Firestone IndyCar 300 at Japan

Film Appearance
2005 *Girl Racers* (herself)

Book
2006 *Danica: Crossing the Line*

Books

Glaser, Jason. *Sports Idols: Danica Patrick*. New York: Rosen Publishing Group, Inc., 2008.

Indy-Tech Publishing Editorial Staff. *Danica Patrick*. Indianapolis, IN: Sams Technical Publishing, LLC, 2006.

Ingram, Jonathan. *Danica Patrick: America's Hottest Racer*. Minneapolis, MN: MBI Publishing Co., 2005.

Mello, Tara Baukus. *Race Car Legends: Danica Patrick*. Philadelphia: Chelsea House Publishers, 2007.

Patrick, Danica, with Laura Morton. *Danica: Crossing the Line*. New York: Fireside, 2006.

Piehl, Janet. *Motor Mania: Indy Race Cars*. Minneapolis, MN: Lerner Publications, 2007.

Savage, Jeff. *Amazing Athletes: Danica Patrick*. Minneapolis, MN: Lerner Publishing Group, 2006.

Web Sites

http://www.danicaracing.com

On Danica Patrick's official site, fans can find her bio and stats, information about her car and sponsors, plus the latest news. Other features include a photo album, streaming video, an online store, and Danica's journal entries.

http://www.indycar.com

The official Web site of the IndyCar Series contains driver bios, photos, news and statistics, rules, car specifications, and more.

http://www.andrettigreenracing.com

The Web site of the Andretti Green Racing team includes a media guide for the current season, with driver information, statistics, and career highlights.

http://www.brickyard.com

The Indianapolis Motor Speedway's Web site features the history of the speedway, Indy 500 traditions and trivia, a schedule of all events held at the Speedway, and more.

http://www.paddocktalk.com

Started in 2004 as a Champ Car news and commentary site, PaddockTalk now hosts editions for IRL, Formula One, NASCAR, Grand Am, and virtually every competitive driving series imaginable. It includes news, forums, photos, and news feeds. TV listings and track maps also help race fans keep on top of all the action in their favorite leagues.

Publisher's note:

The Web sites mentioned in this book were active at the time of publication. The publisher is not responsible for Web sites that have changed their addresses or discontinued operation since the date of publication. The publisher will review and update the Web site addresses each time the book is reprinted.

---

chassis—the frame and working parts of a car underneath the car's body.

developmental races—in auto racing, races set up to promote the growth of drivers until they are ready to race the most powerful cars available against the best competitors.

endorsement—a usually paid recommendation of a product, often by a celebrity.

General Educational Development (GED)—tests that, if passed, enable a student to obtain a high school equivalency diploma without graduating from a traditional high school.

Indy Racing League (IRL)—the sanctioning body for a top-level open-wheel racing series.

morale—mental and emotional feelings of confidence and a sense of purpose.

open-wheel—involving race cars that have no fenders.

pits—the infield area on an automobile racetrack where drivers stop for fuel, new tires, and in-race repairs and maintenance.

pole position—the top starting position for a race, which is on the inside lane of the front row.

suspension—the parts of a car that keep it riding smoothly over bumpy surfaces.

test-drive—to drive a motor vehicle in order to evaluate the vehicle's performance; in racing, a driver's chance to audition for a racing team.

Chapter 1: A Superstar on Wheels

page 6 "I found myself in the position . . ." Danica Patrick with Laura Morton, *Danica: Crossing the Line* (New York: Fireside, 2006), 154.

Chapter 2: Born to Drive

page 12 "Instead of playing soccer . . ." Patrick with Morton, *Danica*, 5.

page 13 "I had no idea . . ." Ibid., 75.

page 14 "Even though it rained . . ." Ibid., 88.

Chapter 3: Making the Big Leagues

page 22 "Daniel Clive Wheldon . . ." Dick Mittman, "Go, Girl: Patrick Makes Statement with Historic Performance," Indianapolis Motor Speedway Web site, May 29, 2005. http://www.indianapolismotor speedway.com/news/print.php?story_id=4737

page 25 "Now that the dust . . ." Patrick with Morton, *Danica*, 50.

Chapter 4: Moving On, Moving Up

page 34 "You just look stupid . . ." A. J. Perez, "Lapped Traffic's Tangles Putting the 'Ire' in IRL," *USA Today*, July 19, 2007. http://www.usatoday.com/sports/motor/irl/2007-07-19-lapped-traffic_N.htm

page 34 "I've never had so many . . ." Ibid.

page 35 "We're going to get . . ." "IRL: Danica Patrick Pre-season Teleconference, Part 1." http://www.motorsport.com/news/article.asp?ID=280311&FS=IRL

Chapter 5: A Life on Track

page 38 "These days I don't . . ." Patrick with Morton, *Danica*, 168.

page 39 "I've had a very good . . ." Associated Press, "Danica to Stay in IRL, but Switch to Andretti Green," July 26, 2006. http://sports.espn.go.com/rpm/news/story?seriesId=1&id=2529364

page 41 "I don't know if . . ." Eric Anderson, "Jenny McCarthy Honored For Efforts Towards Autism," *Access Hollywood*, February 3, 2008. http://www.accesshollywood.com/article/8249/Jenny-McCarthy-Honored-For-Efforts-Towards-Autism/

page 44 "I've bared some skin . . ." Dan Patrick, "Danica Patrick's Q&A," *Sports Illustrated*, Swimsuit 2008. http://sportsillustrated.cnn.com/features/2008_swimsuit/danica-patrick/qa.html

page 44 "Why not use whatever . . ." Patrick with Morton, *Danica*, 137.

page 46 "When Danica passed me . . ." Jim Armstrong, "Victory for Danica Patrick in Japan," *Yahoo! Sports*, April 20, 2008. http://sports.yahoo.com/irl/news?slug=ap-irl-indyjapan300&prov=ap&type=lgns

page 47 "That was a big relief . . ." Ibid.

page 47 "There was a lot of . . ." Ibid.

page 47 "I'm thrilled for her . . ." Ibid.

Cross-Currents

page 52 "I don't really have . . ." Sean Gregory, "10 Questions for Danica Patrick," *Time*, June 5, 2005. http://www.time.com/time/magazine/article/0,9171,1069099,00.html

page 52 "I got firsthand knowledge . . ."
Rusty Wallace, "Wheldon Should Be
Fine; Danica Could Be Awesome,"
ESPN.com, March 27, 2006.
http://sports.espn.go.com/espn/
print?id=2378527&type=story

page 55 "You might call it . . ." Nate Ryan,
"For Patrick, the Question Has Become:
Can She Win?" *USA Today*, May 23,
2007. http://www.usatoday.com/
sports/motor/irl/indy500/2007-
05-23-danica-patrick_N.htm

Kristine Brennan is the author of many books for young readers. She resides in the Philadelphia area.

PICTURE CREDITS

page

1: CSM Photo
4: AJ Mast/Icon SMI
7: Dallas Morning News/MCT
8: Sports Illustrated/NMI
10: Donald Hinkle/CIC Photos
14: Mike Wimmenauer/SPCS
16: Robert Laberge/Getty Images
19: Jonboy/SPCS
20: Indianapolis Star/KRT
23: AP Photo
24: T&T/IOA Photos
26: Worth Canoy/Icon SMI
28: Ron McQueeny/IMS/SPCS
30: SlopeSurfer/SPCS
31: NYSE/FPS

33: Indianapolis Star/KRT
35: AP Photo/Bob Brodbeck
36: Andretti Green Racing/PRMS
39: S. Bailey/CIC Photos
40: Andrew H. Walker/Getty Images
42: Tissot/NMI
43: Evan Agostini/Getty Images
45: Indianapolis Star/KRT
46: Tissot/PRMS
48: IMS Photo Archive
49: Indianapolis Star/KRT
50: Blaues Schiff/IOW Photos
53: Jonboy/SPCS
54: Interstate Bakeries Corp./NMI

Front cover: Rahal Letterman Racing/P&G/PRMS